Contents

Sharks Through Antiquity

From Fear To Fascination

Sharks & Rays

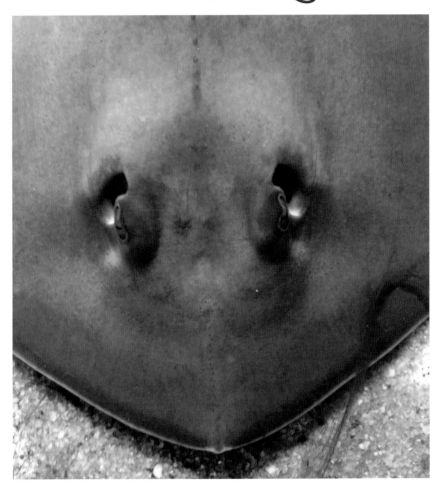

From Fear To Fascination
Sharks & Rays

PART OF THE SEAWORLD EDUCATION SERIES

Research/Writing/Layout
Loran Wlodarski

Technical Advisors
Brad Andrews
Daniel K. Odell
John Kerivan
Pete Mohan
Mike Shaw
Gary Violetta

Editorial Staff
Catherine Gregos
Dennis Jones
Danielle Magee
Deborah Nuzzolo
Patti Schick
Loran Wlodarski

Education Directors
Ann Quinn
William Street
Sheila Voss
Joy L. Wolf

Photos
Mike Aguilera
Bob Couey
Bob French
SeaWorld Orlando Photo
    Services
Loran Wlodarski

Illustrations
Laurie Allen Klein

Cover: A view from below of a sand tiger shark (*Carcharias taurus*).

Title page: A close up of a southern ray (*Dasyatis americana*).

Contents page: Sand tiger sharks as seen through the shark tunnel at SeaWorld San Diego.

Pages iv-1: Up close view of a sand tiger shark.

Pages 10-11: A southern ray glides over another one hidden in the sand.

Pages 34-35: Swell sharks (*Cephaloscyllium ventriosum*) rest in rock crevices. Because they are small, strong currents may pull them away. To prevent this, they "swell" up their stomachs with water and air. As their stomach inflates, they wedge firmly between rocks.

Pages 52-53: A newly hatched brownbanded bamboo shark (*Chiloscyllium plagiosum*) has just emerged from its egg casing.

Published by the SeaWorld Education Department
7007 SeaWorld Drive, Orlando, Florida 32821

ISBN 1–893698–02–5
Printed in the United States of America

"The secret pit of the ocean holds a universe of tangled mysteries."

Joseph MacInnis, ocean explorer

T raveling back in time 400 million years, our planet would appear alien and unfamiliar. No birds or flying insects would fill the sky. On land, there would be no flowering plants to smell. Backboned animals, such as dinosaurs and humans, would not appear for millions of years. But in the sea, there would be sharks.

Sharks have become one of the most successful, adaptive animals on our planet. The earliest evidence of the ancestors of modern sharks comes from the remains of fossilized dorsal fin spines, vertebrae sections, teeth, and scales that appear 350 to 400 million years ago in the Devonian Period, also known as the "Age of Fishes."

One of the earliest shark fossils, *Cladoselache*, was discovered in shale beds near Cleveland, Ohio. Even though this animal roamed the oceans some 400 million years ago, it shared many characteristics of modern sharks such as a torpedo-shaped body and multiple rows of gill slits. It did, however, lack scales over most of its body. The only scales detected on *Cladoselache* were found around the eyes and margins of the fins.

Stethacanthus, a shark of the Late Devonian to Late Carboniferous Period (345 million to 280 million years ago), was quite unusual. Its first dorsal fin was shaped like an anvil and was covered with sharp toothlike structures called denticles. The top part of its head was also covered with denticles, giving it a jagged effect. No one is sure what these features were for, but speculation ranges from use in threat displays to aiding the shark with mating.

Right: A human could easily walk through the open jaws of the ancient megatooth, *Carcharodon megalodon*. This reconstruction is considerably more accurate than early displays, when it was mistakenly thought that megatooth sharks were up to 36.5 m (120 ft.) long—three times longer than what scientists now believe to be its actual length.

As sharks increased their dominance in the oceans, some began invading freshwater rivers and lakes. *Xenacanthus* was one such highly specialized shark. The body was shaped more like an eel, with a continuous dorsal fin down its back, around the tail and joined by the anal fins. Its odd, V-shaped teeth were probably used to seize crustaceans and heavily-scaled fishes. *Xenacanthus* grew one long thick spine from the back of the skull, presumably for protection against other predators.

With teeth the size of a human hand, perhaps the most spectacular of ancient sharks was the megatooth, *Carcharodon megalodon* (which literally means "rough toothed, huge toothed"). After scientific debate over its size, most researchers now believe the megatooth was no longer than 12.4 m (40 ft.). Even at this size, the megatooth still ranks as the largest predatory fish of all time.

The teeth of this shark are triangular, with parallel rows of serrated edges running down the length of both sides. This pattern is duplicated in the great white shark (*Carcharodon carcharias*), although proportionally smaller. Based on similarities between the teeth, researchers believe the two are closely related.

The megatooth was a top predator in warm ocean waters up to 15 million years ago during the Miocene Epoch. During this same time period, whales had reached their peak in diversity and population numbers. These whales were probably a primary food source for the megatooth, as megatooth bite marks can be seen on fossilized vertebrae and other bones of Miocene whales.

Then, during the Pliocene Epoch some 10 million years ago, the earth cooled and large glaciers appeared. Fossil records show these large whales retreated to cooler waters. The combination of glaciers and lack of food may have led to the demise of the mighty megatooth. Yet, unfossilized *Carcharodon megalodon* teeth have been dredged up recently in the Central Pacific Ocean. Could this incredible shark still be alive? With much of the ocean still unexplored, it may be possible.

S harks are a type of fish. Like other fishes, sharks are ectothermic or "cold-blooded," meaning they rely on an outside source to control body temperature. Fishes are backboned creatures that use gills to get oxygen from the water and use fins for swimming. Living fish species are separated into three classes:

- *Agnatha*, or jawless fishes. These extremely primitive fishes have fossils that can be traced back 520 million years. They were the first type of fish and the first known vertebrate animals. They lack a jaw and a skeleton made of bone. Instead, their skeletons are composed of cartilage. Some scientists replace Agnatha with the class Myxini (hagfishes) and the class Cephalaspidomorphi (lampreys).

Unlike these lookdown fish (*Selene vomer*), sharks lack bones. Red blood cells in sharks are therefore produced in the kidneys and epigonal organ. White blood cells are produced in the spleen and spiral valve within the intestine.

- *Chondrichthyes*, or cartilaginous fishes. Chondrichthyan fishes have a skeleton of cartilage, jaws, paired fins, and paired nostrils. Granules of calcium carbonate on the outside of the cartilage add strength. These fishes also lack a swim bladder found in most bony fishes. Chondrichthyes includes the subclasses Holocephali and Elasmobranchii.

Chimaeras are in the Chondrichthyes subclass Holocephali. They are characterized by having no scales, one pair of gill openings, and an upper jaw that is fused to the cranium (brain casing). Sharks, stingrays, electric rays, manta rays, skates, guitarfishes, and sawfishes are in the subclass Elasmobranchii. They have multiple rows of gill openings (five to seven pairs), placoid scales, and an upper jaw that is not fused to the cranium.

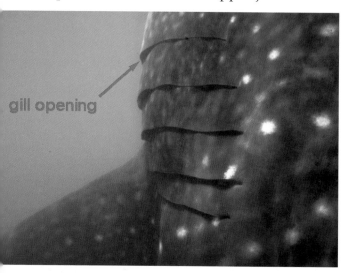

gill opening

A close-up of the five gill openings of a whale shark (*Rhincodon typus*). All sharks have five gill opening pairs, except for sharks in the order Hexanchiformes (which have six or seven pairs) and the sixgill sawshark (*Pliotrena warreni*).

Batoidea is the superorder comprised of rays, skates, guitarfishes, and sawfishes. There are about 480 batoid species separated into four orders. The 355 or so shark species are in the superorder Selachii. Sharks are further divided into eight orders and 30 families (see pages 68–69 for a complete list of elasmobranch groupings). Most shark families have remained virtually unchanged for the past 100 million years.

- *Osteichthyes*, or bony fishes. The bony fish class represents the most successful group of all vertebrates, accounting for 96% of all living fish species and half of all vertebrates. There are approximately 23,500 bony fish species. All share a skeleton made up of hard bone, one pair of gill openings, paired fins, jaws, and paired nostrils. Most have scales, although none have placoid scales found on chondrichthyan fishes.

R ays, skates, guitarfishes, and sawfishes resemble sharks in many ways. There are a few differences, one of the most noteworthy being the placement of their gill openings. Sharks have five to seven pairs of gill openings are on both sides of their heads. Batoids and sawfishes have five or six pairs underneath their bodies. They also have expanded pectoral fins fused to their heads.

Of the rays, skates, and sawfishes, rays were the first to develop, beginning in the Late Jurassic Period, some 150 million years ago. Remains of *Spathobathis*, the earliest known ray, were discovered in France and Germany. Since then, rays have diversified to both fresh and oceanic environments around the world.

Stingrays grow one or more spines at the base of their tail. This sharp, venomous barb has serrated edges that point backward, making it difficult to remove when it is impaled into a victim. The barb is for defense; not to gather food or attack. If a ray loses a barb, it can grow back similar to the way that human fingernails regrow. During that growth period, however, the ray is vulnerable to predation.

As their name implies, stingrays, like this spotted eagle ray (*Aetobatus narinari*), possess a formidable defensive barb. It contains a potent venom that can cause symptoms ranging from painful skin swelling to death in humans.

stingray barb

Stingrays spend a great deal of time buried under sand, for their primary defense is to hide from predators. Humans occasionally step on and hurt these unseen rays when at the beach. When this happens, these rays attempt to maneuver their tail around to sting. To avoid this scenario, humans walking along the shore should do the "stingray shuffle." By kicking around the sand in shallow waters, rays are alerted to the presence of a threat and may move out of the way.

Southern stingrays (*Dasyatis americana*) are well camouflaged when buried under sand in shallow water.

Another defense developed by some rays is the ability to deliver a powerful electric shock. All living organisms produce low levels of electricity, but these rays have special organs which act as living batteries. Located in the front of their bodies, one to each side, the lower sections of these organs have a negative charge while the top is positively charged. With up to a million generating units between the two organs, some species, such as numb electric rays (*Torpedo nobiliana*), can shock victims with 220 volts; twice the standard current that flows through a house in the United States.

Manta rays rely on another defense entirely — size. Their incredible wingspan of up to 7.5 m (25 ft.) and weight up to 1,360 kg (3,000 lb.) is great enough to keep most predators away. Despite their monstrous appearance, manta rays are gentle, plankton feeding animals that pose no real threat to humans.

Skates resemble rays in many ways, but rays give live birth to their pups while skates lay eggs. Beachgoers sometimes find empty skate egg cases, called "mermaid's purses," washed up on the shore.

A sawfish has a flattened rostrum (snout) which can be longer than 2 m (6.5 ft.) and is lined with a row of sharp teeth on each side. A sawfish may swing its rostrum back

The snout of the smalltooth sawfish (*Pristis pectinata*) is a valuable souvenir on the black market.

and forth while swimming through a school of fish, injuring them from the impact. A sawfish's mouth is under its body, and this positioning allows a sawfish to eat injured fish that sink to the bottom. Sawfishes have also been seen using their snout teeth to move sand around in search of food.

Sawsharks, which are superficially similar to sawfishes, are true sharks while sawfishes are not. Sawfishes have gill slits located on the ventral side of their bodies while sawsharks have gill slits on their sides. Sawsharks also have rostrum teeth alternating in size from large to small, and long, fingerlike barbels hanging from the rostrum.

Shovelnose guitarfish (*Rhinobatus productus*) often bury themselves under sand for protection like many other batoids.

Another strange shark relative is the guitarfish. This passive animal relies on its ability to hide from predators under sand. Some, such as the shovelnose guitarfish, can obtain a length of 1.5 m (5 ft.) or more. Like rays, the mouth of a guitarfish is under its body as it too is a bottom feeder.

9

Perfect Predators

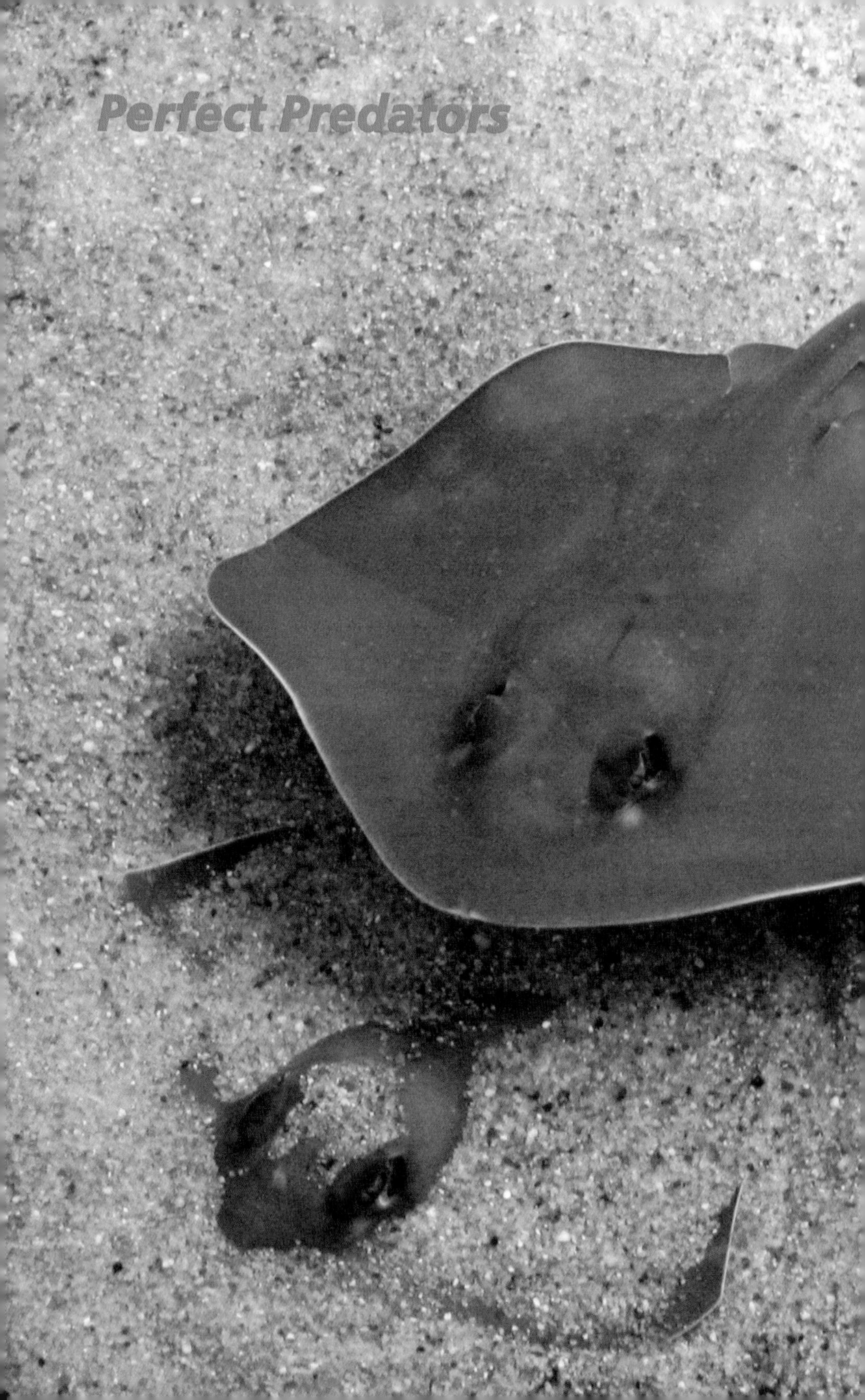

"An ocean full of sharks is a healthy ocean."

Animal adventurers Chris and Martin Kratt

S harks are equipped with an array of advanced senses. Perhaps the most well known is their ability to smell. Sharks have often been described as "swimming noses," and with good reason. Some sharks have two-thirds of their brain weight devoted to smell. As a shark swims or takes water in through its mouth to breathe, some of the water passes in and out of each nasal sac. A shark's sense of smell functions up to hundreds of meters away from a source. Sharks can locate minute quantities of substances such as blood in the water. In experiments, sharks could detect a concentration as low as one part per billion of some chemicals, such as certain amino acids.

In one test, sharks were placed in an aquarium next to another which was filled with bony fish. Neither shark nor fish could see one another, although a set of small connecting pipes allowed water to flow through to each aquarium. At first, the sharks were not interested in the fish. Then, the fish were agitated by researchers. The sharks suddenly became interested in the fish, swimming close to the pipes to investigate. The sharks may have been attracted by excessive movements in the water or chemicals released by the fish during their agitated state.

Some sharks have whisker-like flaps called barbels near their nostril area. The mandarin dogfish (*Cirrhigaleus barbifer*) trails its long barbels on the ocean floor to find prey, just as a catfish does. Presumably the barbels may enhance tactile or chemoreception. This feature can be found on other species such as sawsharks and nurse sharks.

barbe

Barbels on the nurse shark (*Ginglymostoma cirratum*) may help it locate food.

Humans have long discounted the eyesight of sharks, believing it to be poor. In reality, sharks have well-developed eyes. In clear water, a shark's vision is effective up to about 15 m (50 ft.).

Unlike most other fish, sharks have pupils that dilate and contract. This gives sharks the advantage of adjusting their eyesight to both bright and dim light. Some sharks are still very sensitive to light, such as the puffadder shysharks (*Haploblepharus edwardsii*) of South Africa. When plucked out of the water by humans, shysharks curl their tails back in an attempt to cover their eyes. Blind sharks (*Brachaelurus waddi*) are not visually impaired, as their name implies, but they firmly shut their eyes to avoid sunlight when pulled out of the water.

Eye size and position vary among sharks, depending on habitat and behavior. In general, deep-water sharks have larger eyes than shallow-water sharks. Bigeye thresher sharks (*Alopias superciliosus*) have their eyes directed upward, perhaps because they encircle schools of fishes above them. The odd looking hammerhead and bonnethead sharks (family Sphyrnidae) have eyes and nostrils set on either side of their characteristic hammer-shaped heads. This may give them an advantage of seeing and smelling a wide area with little effort.

Sharks have a basic vertebrate eye, although it is somewhat flattened. The lens is large and spherical and the eyes contain both rod and cone cells. There is a greater proportion of rod cells, which are highly sensitive to changes in light intensity, making sharks sensitive to contrasts of light and shadow. Cone cells indicate that sharks may have color vision, although more studies are needed to determine the extent of this. Behind the retina, the eye has a layer of reflective plates called the tapetum lucidum. These plates act as mirrors to reflect light back through the retina a second time. The tapetum lucidum is twice as effective as that of a cat. In bright light, pigments temporarily cover and block the tapetum to prevent eye damage from intense sunlight.

Sharks have well-developed eyes that can possibly see colors.

To protect their eyes when biting down on thrashing prey, some sharks roll their eyes back as they bite. Others have a structure called a nictitating membrane which covers the eye like an eyelid.

Perhaps the least studied shark sense is taste. Taste buds in a shark's mouth may be responsible for a shark's final acceptance or rejection of food items. Some sharks seem to prefer certain foods over others and have been known to spit out things that may have had an unpleasant taste.

Sensory pits are distributed in large numbers on the backs, flanks, and lower jaws of sharks. These sensory pits are formed by the overlapping of two enlarged scales guarding a slight depression in the skin. At the bottom of the pit is a sensory papilla: a small cluster of sensory cells that resembles a taste bud. The function of these sensory pits has not been determined. They may be organs that are stimulated by physical factors such as water current.

Under water, sound travels about four and half times faster than through air so sound is often the first sense a shark relies on to locate prey. Sharks have only an inner ear, which consists of three chambers and an ear stone called an otolith. A shark's inner ear detects sound, acceleration, and gravity. Sharks are attracted to low-frequency pulsed sounds, like the erratic sounds made by wounded animals. Most attractive sounds are in the frequency of 25 to 100 Hz. Some sharks are attracted to sound sources from distances as great as 250 m (820 ft.).

Fishes have a lateral line system consisting of a series of fluid-filled canals just below the skin on the head and along the sides of their bodies. The canals are open to the surrounding water through tiny pores. The lateral line canals contain a number of sensory cells called neuromasts. Tiny hairlike structures on the neuromasts project into the canal. Water movement created by turbulence, currents, or vibrations displaces these hairlike projections and stimulates the neuromasts. This stimulation triggers a nerve impulse to the brain. Like the ear, the lateral line senses low-frequency vibrations. It also functions in distance perception and detecting the direction of water flow.

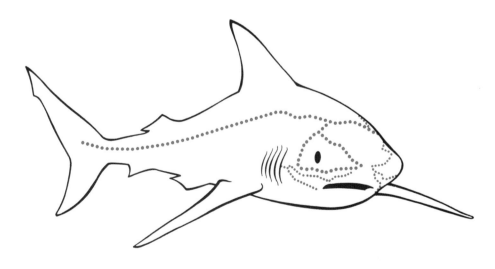

The lateral line is a series of fluid-filled canals.

Bonnethead sharks (*Sphyrna tiburo*) have an unusual placement for their eyes and nostrils. By moving their elongated heads slightly, they are able to see and smell in a wide area.

Sharks also possess a sense not found in most animals; the ability to detect electrical currents through a complex system called the ampullae of Lorenzini. These external pores cover the surface of a shark's head. Each pore leads to a jelly-filled canal which then goes into a membranous sac called an ampulla. In the wall of the ampulla are sensory cells with nerve fibers that can detect weak electrical fields at short distances. As mentioned earlier, sharks probably protect their eyes when they feed, making them unable to see their prey as they strike. The ampullae of Lorenzini may guide them in the final stages of prey capture.

Great hammerhead sharks (*Sphyrna mokarran*) tend to hunt stingrays (one great hammerhead was found with about 50 barb injuries in its mouth, throat and tongue). Its large head has more surface area for additional ampullae of Lorenzini. Great hammerheads may use their elongated heads like a minesweeper, swinging it back and forth over the sand to find buried rays. This, combined with the wide placement of their eyes and nostrils, makes great hammerheads superior hunters.

Mainly considered electroreceptors, scientists theorize that ampullae of Lorenzini also detect salinity, temperature, changes in water pressure, and mechanical stimuli. These sensors also may help orient sharks with electromagnetic fields surrounding the Earth. This may explain why some shark species are able to travel long migration routes on a regular basis.

M ost sharks have a fusiform body shape (cylindrical and tapering at both ends), like an elongated football. This type of body design reduces drag and requires less energy to swim compared to sea animals without a fusiform shape. Sharks have various rigid fins along their bodies. Fins, which are supported by cartilaginous rods, help stabilize or propel a fish in the water.

Most sharks have two dorsal fins to stabilize them as they swim. The lemon shark (*Negaprion brevirostris*) is one of the few species that have both dorsal fins approximately the same size. For most sharks the first dorsal fin is generally taller than the second. Others, like primitive frilled sharks (*Chlamydoselachus anguineus*), have only one dorsal fin. Piked dogfish (*Squalus acanthias*) have dorsal spines equipped with an irritating venom. When threatened, piked dogfish curl up and whip their longer second dorsal spine towards an enemy. The toxin can cause painful, allergic reactions in humans.

Some smaller shark species like this horn shark (*Heterodontus francisci*) have sharp spines on each dorsal fin for protection against predators.

Paired pectoral fins control steering and add lift as the shark swims. The tail, or caudal fin, has an upper lobe always longer than the lower lobe. This caudal fin design creates a downward thrust to balance the lift produced by the pectoral fins, thus a shark can stay straight while swimming. The caudal fin lobes of porbeagle sharks (*Lamna nasus*) are nearly symmetrical, allowing them to achieve greater swimming speeds. Bottom dwelling nurse sharks hunt slow-moving prey for the most part, so they do not require great bursts of speed to capture prey like porbeagle sharks. The lower caudal lobes of nurse sharks are virtually non-existent.

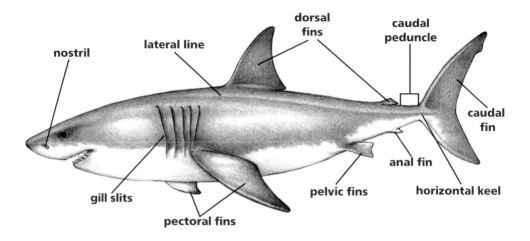

An external look at a great white shark.

Paired pelvic fins and a single anal fin also help stabilize a shark as it swims. Some sharks, such as the dumb gulper shark (*Centrophorus harrissoni*), lack an anal fin.

Sharks propel themselves forward by moving their caudal fin from side to side and their backbone extends all the way through the caudal fin for added power. Sharks cannot move backwards. Although capable of short bursts of speed, most sharks are generally not fast moving. Some cruise the waters at only 5 kph (about 3 mph). Shortfin makos (*Isurus oxyrinchus*) rank among the fastest, with top speeds reaching up to 48 kph (30 mph). Some characteristics distinguishing a fast moving shark include a fusiform body shape, a caudal fin with nearly equal lobes, smoother skin than a typical shark, and the presence of a horizontal keel (although a few slow-moving species like the whale shark also possess a horizontal keel). The horizontal keel reduces turbulence and is found on the caudal peduncle of a few sharks.

Fast-swimming sharks, such as makos, are active enough to have body temperatures higher than the surrounding water; nearly unheard of in cold-blooded animals. With muscle temperatures of up to 8° C (14.4° F) above the surrounding water, these sharks are sometimes referred to as "warm-bodied" fishes.

Sharks: an Inside Look

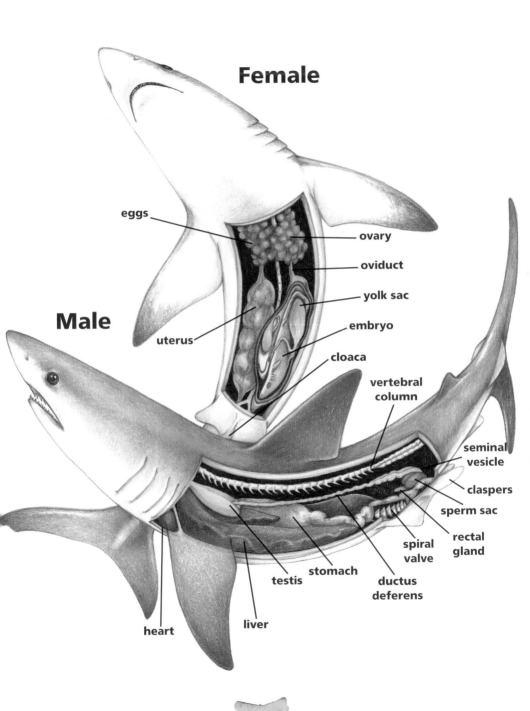

Female

Male

eggs

ovary

oviduct

yolk sac

uterus

embryo

cloaca

vertebral
column

seminal
vesicle

claspers

sperm sac

rectal
gland

spiral
valve

ductus
deferens

testis

stomach

liver

heart

Most bony fishes have a gas filled sac called a swim bladder which helps them float. A shark lacks a swim bladder, making it heavier than water. Most sharks will sink if they stop swimming. Sand tiger sharks (*Carcharias taurus*) are the exceptions. They gulp air at the surface, filling their stomachs with air which adds buoyancy to their bodies.

A large liver, in addition to storing energy for periods of time when sharks cannot find food, helps a shark compensate for the lack of a swim bladder. The two-lobed liver of a shark is filled with oil. Oil, being lighter than water, adds buoyancy to sharks. A shark's liver makes up 5% to 25% of its total body weight and takes up to 90% of the space inside its body cavity. A great white shark weighing 3,312 kg (7,302 lb.) had a liver 456 kg (1,005 lb.) in weight. Basking sharks (*Cetorhinus maximus*) have an exceptionally high concentration of oil in their livers. One large specimen had a liver that yielded 2,270 liters (549 gallons) of oil, for example.

Sharks and their relatives have placoid scales, also called dermal denticles ("skin teeth"). Placoid scales consist of an outer layer of vitro-dentine (an enamel), dentine, and a pulp cavity. Placoid scales are arranged in regular patterns in sharks and irregular patterns in their batoid relatives. In theory, these scales gave rise to teeth in a fish's mouth, as well as stingray barbs and dorsal spines on some types of sharks. As a shark continues to grow it produces more placoid scales.

Sharks are covered on nearly every part of their bodies with placoid scales, giving them added protection from predators. Some species have large and formidable dermal denticles, especially bramble sharks (*Echinorhinus brucus*) and prickly sharks (*Echinorhinus cookei*). Bramble sharks have thornlike placoid spikes on their bodies, some in plates measuring 25 mm (nearly one inch) across. But, what some sharks gain in protection they lose to water drag. The drag on a brown shark (*Carcharhinus plumbeus*) is known to be up to ten times greater than on the smooth and sleek skin of a dolphin.

A close inspection of placoid scales shows that they run in consistent patterns; the sharper end usually points towards the tail, although some denticles have sharp points in numerous directions. If a diver were to touch a shark from its head to its tail, he or she would notice that the skin may feel rough. But if the diver went the opposite way, against the grain of the scales, it is possible that the dermal denticles could abrade a diver's wetsuit and skin.

Some sharks have greatly reduced placoid scales. This may allow for a series of vortices or whirlpools to be created behind each scale. As the names would suggest, an angular roughshark (*Oxynotus centrina*) has a different feeling skin than a narrownose smoothhound (*Mustelus punctulatus*). Because dermal denticles are unique for every shark, they are used by scientists to identify various species.

Many shark species (such as catsharks in the family Scyliorhinidae) have noticeably larger and sharper dermal denticles that are often visible to the human eye.

A whale shark can be easily identified by its checkerboard skin pattern of yellowish stripes and dots and for its titanic size, which averages 4 m to 12 m (13–39 ft.) in length. It is believed they can reach a maximum size of 18 m (59 ft.) with a weight of around 11,800 kg (26,000 lb.). The smallest free-swimming whale shark seen was 56 cm (22 in.), which may be close to its hatching size.

The second-largest species of fish is the basking shark. Most do not grow larger than 9.8 m (32 ft.), but some reach a maximum size of 12.2 to 15.2 m (40–50 ft.). As with most shark species, females grow about 25% larger than the males. There are some exceptions to this general rule, such as male catsharks in the genus *Holohalaelurus*, which can get a few centimeters longer than the females.

Top: The whitespotted bambooshark (*Chiloscyllium plagiosum*) is a small shark species. Adults range in size from 67 to 95 cm (26–37 in.), which is only slightly bigger than a newborn whale shark.

Left: Whale sharks can be as big as two school buses or more.

Many times, shark sizes are exaggerated or unable to be verified. A stranded great white shark off New Brunswick, Canada, was said to have been 11.3 m (37 ft.) long, although it was not scientifically confirmed. A great white caught in the Azores in 1978 was said to be 9 m (29.5 ft.) in length. The largest great white officially weighed was a 6.4-m (21-ft.) specimen caught near Cuba in 1945. It weighed 3,312 kg (7,302 lb.). Great whites that have been caught by fishermen range from 1.4 to 6 m (4.6–20 ft.) long.

Only 39 shark species are known to grow larger than 3 m (10 ft.) while 176 species measure less than 1 m (39 in.). The spined pygmy shark (*Squaliolus laticaudus*) is probably the smallest of all sharks. Females reach about 18 cm (7.1 in.) in length while mature males may only be 15 cm (5.9 in.) long. The pygmy ribbontail catshark (*Eridacnis radcliffei*), with a maximum size of 24 cm (9.5 in.), is only slightly longer.

For some species, markings change as a shark ages. Young zebra sharks (*Stegostoma fasciatum*), for example, are born with dark bands and saddles that fade to rather uniformly distributed spots on the adults. As adults, they are often referred to as Australian leopard sharks.

Coloration helps some sharks blend in with their ocean environment. Juvenile tiger sharks (*Galeocerdo cuvieri*), while they are young and more vulnerable, have stripes for camouflage. These stripes fade considerably as they grow.

The coloration of a shark plays other important roles for its survival. Countershading is a type of coloration in which the dorsal (top) side is darker than the ventral (bottom) side. In general, most sharks are drably countershaded. The dark top of a countershaded animal blends in with the dark ocean depths when viewed from above. The lighter ventral side blends in with the lighter surface of the water when viewed from below. The result is that predators or prey do not easily distinguish a contrast between the countershaded animal and the environment.

Epaulette sharks (*Hemiscyllium ocellatum*) grow to a maximum

length of 107 cm (42 in.). Because they are relatively small and may fall prey to larger predators, epaulettes have developed a "false eye" on the sides of their bodies. From a distance, the false eyes may fool predators into thinking epaulettes are much larger.

In French, epaulette means "shoulder patch," a reference to this shark's large false eye patches.

Wobbegong sharks (family Orectolobidae) and angelsharks (family Squatinidae) are flatter than most sharks. Combined with a mottled or sandy skin coloration, these sharks are camouflaged on the ocean floor. Like a stingray, some bury themselves under sand or mud, leaving only their eyes and the top of their bodies exposed.

Wobbegong sharks are flat in shape.

Some shark species are bioluminescent: they glow in the dark. Bioluminescence can be an adaptation for concealment or for countershading and for gathering food. Lanternsharks (family Squalidae) secrete a glowing mucus on their bodies. The cookiecutter shark, whose genus *Isistius* is named after the Egyptian goddess of light, emits a bright green glow from its belly. The taillight shark (*Euprotomicroides zantedeschia*) has a special gland on its underside that secretes a luminous blue substance. The spined pygmy shark has dense photophores covering its ventral surface but little or none on its sides or top of the body. This bioluminescent pattern has been described as "photophore countershading." On a moonlit night, fish swimming through the water would normally produce a shadow that predators would see. The glowing underside of lantern sharks reduces or eliminates this shadow, making them less conspicuous to predators.

Glowing bacteria surrounds the mouth of the megamouth shark (*Megachasma pelagios*). The glow may attract tiny shrimp into its gaping jaw. Greenland sharks (*Somniosus microcephalus*) have a glowing copepod (a crustacean parasite) that attaches itself to the cornea of each eye. The effect of the glow may attract prey, but the true relationship between the shark and copepods has not been well studied.

Unlike many bony fish species, it is easy to identify male and female sharks. Male sharks have claspers, which are modified inner edges of the pelvic fins adapted for transferring sperm to the female shark. Claspers are unique to cartilaginous fishes.

Smaller species may reach sexual maturity in as few as three or four years. Larger species like dusky sharks (*Carcharhinus obscurus*) grow slowly and may not reach maturity for 15 years or longer.

The exact stimulus to promote male mating behaviors is unknown, but it is thought that the female releases a chemical pheromone when she is ready to breed.

During mating, males of many species bite females on the pectoral fins or the middle of the back to hold onto them. In some elasmobranchs, males have longer, narrower teeth than females. Females often bear scars and marks from breeding. In some species, such as blue sharks, the skin on the back and flanks of the females is more than twice as thick as the skin on the males.

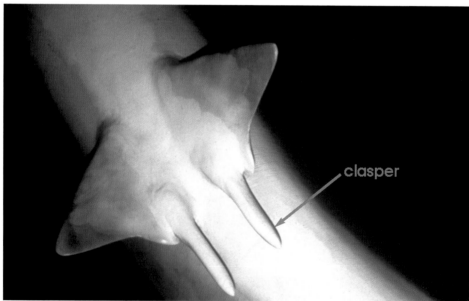
clasper

Claspers are modified inner edges of the pelvic fins.

Bonnethead sharks give live birth to their young. Shark pups are fully functional and ready to survive when born.

During copulation, the erectile claspers are bent forward. In larger, more rigid species the male positions himself parallel and head-to-head with the female. In smaller, more flexible species the male coils himself around the female. The male then inserts one clasper at a time into the female. In some species, claspers contain cartilaginous hooks, or spurs, that dig into the walls of the female oviduct, "clasping" it in place. Seminal fluid is forced down a groove in the clasper and into the female oviduct. Just as males have two claspers, females possess two oviducts.

Elasmobranch eggs are fertilized internally. This form of reproduction may give the sharks an advantage over the majority of bony fishes that spawn by releasing eggs and sperm randomly into the water. External fertilization requires great quantities of egg and sperm production. Internal fertilization is a key adaptation for energy-intensive reproduction.

Gestation periods vary greatly among species and between individuals within a species. Sharks and rays, generally being ectothermic, have no exact gestation time. The rate at which the embryos develop depends on the water temperature. The warmer the water, the quicker the development. In general, most embryos develop somewhere in the range of two months (for some rays) to possibly years. The piked dogfish has a gestation period that may last 18 to 24 months, perhaps the longest of any vertebrate animal.

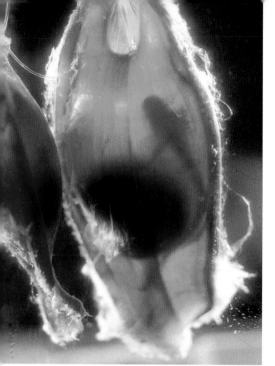

Left: A shark egg case shows a tiny embryo attached to a yolk.
Top right: An epaulette shark pup emerges from its egg.
Bottom right: The horn shark lays spiral egg cases.

Some researchers, however, believe basking sharks have a gestation period of three and a half years.

After internal fertilization, there are three types of embryonic development that may occur. In oviparous ("egg birth") sharks, a gland secretes a shell, or case, around the egg as it passes through the oviduct. The mother deposits the protective egg cases into the sea. When the egg is first laid, it is soft and pale but the case hardens and darkens within a few hours. Inside the egg, the developing embryo receives nutrients from a yolk formed prior to fertilization. Oviparous sharks include horn and bamboo sharks.

Some eggs have spiral fringes to help wedge into rocks and cracks while others may have tendrils on the sides to hook onto sea vegetation. Port Jackson sharks (*Heterodontus portusjacksoni*) carry their egg cases in their mouths, possibly to drop them in a hiding spot. This is about the only shark parental care observed by humans.

In ovoviviparous ("egg live birth") sharks, the shell is often just a thin membrane. Sometimes there is more than one egg in a membrane; this group of eggs is called a candle. The mother retains the egg, and the embryo soon sheds the membrane and develops in the mother's uterus. In theory, all of the embryo's nutrients come from the yolk. In some species, however, the uterine lining may secrete nutritive fluids that the embryo absorbs. An amazing example of ovoviviparous birth comes from the pygmy ribbontail catshark. Although the females mature at 16 cm (6 in.), they produce one or two young that can be 11 cm (4 in.) long.

Recently, whale sharks have been confirmed to be ovoviviparous, but based on an egg recovered in the Gulf of Mexico, whale sharks were once thought to simply lay eggs. The egg measured an astonishing 30 cm (12 in.) long, 14 cm (5.5 in.) wide and 9 cm (3.5 in.) thick, making it the biggest egg of any animal ever seen.

In some species, like sand tiger sharks, embryos continue to obtain nutrients after their yolk is absorbed by swallowing eggs and smaller embryos in the uterus. This is called "intrauterine cannibalism" or ovophagy ("egg eating"). In these sharks, usually only one embryo survives in each of the two uteri. False catsharks (*Pseudotriakis microdon*) are believed to produce 20,000 eggs in each ovary, yet litters of only two to four pups are born at a time. Intrauterine cannibalism may partially explain the disappearance of the other eggs, but this hypothesis has not been proven.

In viviparous ("live birth") sharks, the yolk stalk that connects the embryo grows long in the uterus. Where the small yolk sac comes in contact with the uterus, it changes into a yolk sac "placenta." Nutrients needed by the embryo are passed directly from the tissues of the mother to the tissues of the developing embryo. In addition, the uterine lining secretes "uterine milk," which bathes the developing embryo. The branched yolk sac absorbs this fluid. When the embryo is fully developed, it is born live into the water. Viviparous sharks include hammerhead, bull, and lemon sharks.

Greenland sharks' scientific name, *Somniosus microcephalus*, means "sleepy little head." Sharks are often seen motionless on the sea floor, but do they sleep? Probably not. If they did, predators could easily attack them. Instead of sleeping, many sharks probably rest while staying at least in a semi-conscious state. No open ocean (pelagic) sharks have been seen resting on the ocean floor, although this does not mean that all sharks must constantly swim to survive. Some active species like bull and gray reef sharks (*Carcharhinus amblyrhynchos*) have been seen resting on the ocean bottom. Species ranging from tiny whitespotted bamboo sharks to the 4.3 m (14 ft.) long Pacific sleeper shark (*Somniosus pacificus*) frequent the ocean floor. Resting conserves energy and is a way for some small species to avoid predators.

Nurse sharks can often be found resting together in groups.

Sharks that rest for extended periods of time on the sea floor usually have small openings called spiracles located behind their eyes. These openings bring oxygen-carrying water into the gill chamber. Spiracles originated from rudimentary gill slits and are reduced or absent in fast-swimming sharks.

Sharks have low blood pressure. The walls of the pericardium (the membranous sac that encloses the heart) are rigid, creating a suction within the pericardium to maintain the flow of blood. Even if a shark is resting on an ocean substrate, it must occasionally swing its tail to create muscular contractions needed to circulate its blood.

It was once assumed that to respire all sharks must swim constantly to move water into their mouth and over their gills. It is now known that some sharks can pump water over their gills by opening and closing their mouths. Lemon sharks do this when they stop swimming. Strangely, it takes more energy for the lemon shark to force water through its mouth and over the gills than to continue swimming. No one is sure why they choose to rest on the ocean floor from time to time.

A shark that continuously swims throughout its life periodically rests by using a swim/glide pattern of movement. After the shark swings its tail, it simply glides through the water for a moment. The shark continues this swim/glide pattern during the time it is resting.

Shark exhibits at SeaWorld Adventure Parks are designed to accommodate shark swim/glide patterns. Corners are eliminated because they create an energy burden on the shark to get out of a corner, while long straight sections permit the sharks to glide and rest.

I f sharks of the same species swim together, they are usually all about the same size. There is a good reason for this. Many large sharks eat smaller sharks, even those of their own species. Since females are larger than males in most species, the two sexes normally stay separated as well. Pregnant females may also isolate themselves so their pups are more protected from the males. In the daily struggle for life in the ocean, a main natural predator of a shark is probably another shark.

Sharks are known to be hosts to all sorts of parasites ranging from sea lice to tapeworms. Many creatures assist sharks by removing these parasites, such as banded coral shrimp (*Stenopus hispidus*), cleaner wrasses (*Labroides* spp.), butterflyfishes, angelfishes, and gobies.

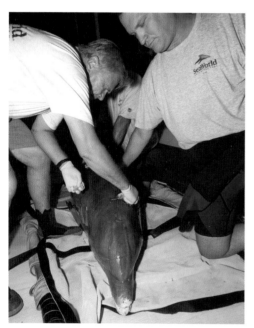

Sharks occasionally prey on bottlenose dolphins (*Tursiops truncatus*) and other cetaceans. This dolphin was rescued by SeaWorld after it had been injured by a shark bite near its head.

Contrary to popular belief, a pod of dolphins near a beach is no guarantee that sharks will not be in the area. In fact, if there is a bountiful supply of food such as a school of fish, dolphins and sharks have been seen feeding near each other. A healthy, adult dolphin can probably defend itself well against a shark, or flee if necessary. Yet certain sharks do feed on dolphins. A great white, bull, or a tiger shark will attack dolphins but they would most likely prey on the young, weak, or sick.

Most sharks would avoid killer whales. For one reason, sharks tend to travel by themselves while killer whales enjoy the protection of their pod.

Killer whales (*Orcinus orca*) are the largest predators of vertebrate animals in the sea. In 1997, a conflict between a great white shark and killer whale was captured on film, although it was not much of a fight. A killer whale female mauled the smaller great white in front of her calf, perhaps for protection or to teach the young whale how to hunt. The footage is no indication of the outcome of every encounter between these two top predators.

Accompanying sharks may be pilotfish (*Naucrates ductor*) and remoras (family Echeneidae). It was once thought that pilotfish led sharks to their next meal, but this is not the case. Pilotfish may travel with sharks to eat scraps of food when sharks feed, or to save energy by riding the hydrodynamic wake of the shark. Probably the only thing that saves pilotfish from becoming the shark's next meal is their speed and agility. Remoras commonly attach themselves to sharks, probably to catch a free ride or to eat parasites on the shark's body.

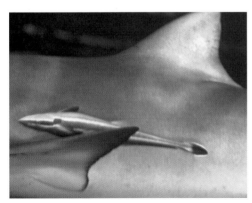

A remora's dorsal fin is a modified sucking disc which it uses to attach itself to large animals.

Diving Into
Diets

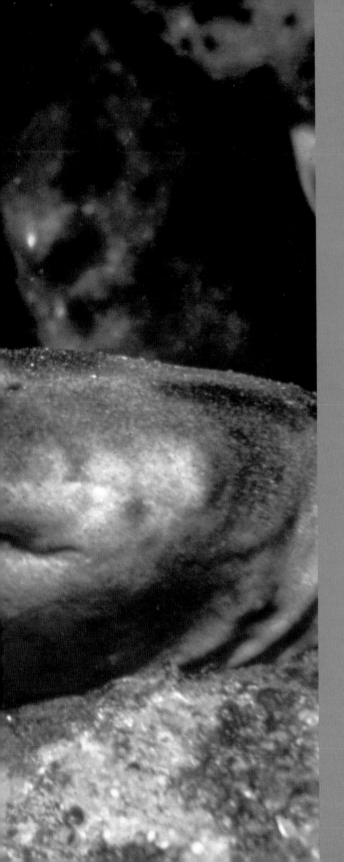

"It grows to a considerable size. It is said that in the belly of one of those monsters, an entire human body was once found, which is far from improbable, considering their love for human flesh."

French scientist Thomas Pennant in a 1776 report on great white sharks

From the largest baleen whales to the smallest zooplankton, sharks have found ways to capitalize on the immense bounty of food that is found in or near the ocean. They even occasionally eat refuse dumped into the sea by humans; items ranging from bottles of wine to license plates have been found inside the stomachs of sharks. Nothing exemplifies this more than tiger sharks, sometimes called "garbage can sharks" for their habit of eating just about anything. Tiger sharks are highly opportunistic when it comes to feeding, but they tend to concentrate their efforts on marine reptiles. Not only do they consume sea turtles, but they are one of only a few animals that prey upon highly venomous sea snakes.

Pygmy sharks (*Euprotomicrus bispinatus*) go to great lengths to find their next meal. They begin their journey at the bottom of the ocean some 1,800 m (5,900 ft.) deep. Then it is believed they travel some 1,500 m (4,920 ft.) up and down each night to feed. This is the equivalent of a human climbing 11 km (nearly seven miles) up and down each day to eat.

Left and above: Sharks at SeaWorld are given a complete physical every six months to assess growth rates, pregnancies, and overall health. The sharks are kept healthy by hand feeding them several times a week. By feeding the sharks one at a time, the SeaWorld staff ensures each shark eats a well-balanced and complete meal.

Just about any animal in the ocean can be a meal to a shark. Great whites prey on California sea lions, wobbegongs eat shrimp, and tiger sharks feed on several species of sea turtles.

Sharks have U-shaped stomachs that lead into the intestine which is coiled into a spiral valve to increase surface area and nutrient absorption. If a shark eats something terribly upsetting, some species can force their stomach out through their mouth and into the water to empty it out. A few sharks have highly specialized stomachs. If threatened, the balloon shark (*Cephlaloscyllium sufflans*) can rapidly inflate its stomach with air or water just like pufferfish and porcupinefish.

Cookiecutters (*Isistius brasiliensis*) are one of the oddest types of sharks. Although only reaching a maximum size of around 50 cm (20 in.), cookiecutters are parasitic predators. They have one of the highest ratios of tooth to body size, and they use their razor-sharp teeth to bite into a victim, twist around and gouge out a cookie-shaped disc of flesh. SeaWorld has rescued injured animals, such as sea lions and whales, with cookiecutter bites. Bites have also been found on submarine listening devices. It is believed the sharks mistook submarines for whales. Rare among sharks, cookiecutters have a highly calcified skeletal structure to support their active lifestyle.

Another extraordinary example of feeding comes from the bigeye thresher shark. The upper tail lobe of this shark can be up to 40% of its total body length, and it uses its tail to encircle and herd schools of fish into a tight group. This makes it easier to charge into the fish group and feed. The bigeye thresher shark also uses its tail to hit and stun small fish. Bigeye threshers are one of the few shark species known to cooperatively hunt for fish.

Some sharks even come out of the water to attack prey on land. Tiger sharks swim onto sandy beaches to capture a variety of animals such as sea turtles and birds. Smoothhound sharks sometimes hurl themselves onto muddy shores to feed on crabs. These sharks must wiggle their way back into the water when their prey is captured.

Adult killer whales commonly eat 3% to 4% of their body weight daily, California sea lions consume 5% to 8% daily, manatees eat around 10% every day, and sea otters put away an astonishing 20% to 30% of their body weight in food every day. These warm-blooded animals require a high level of energy to maintain a constant body temperature. The human body is like a furnace, needing a great deal of "fuel," or food, to keep a body temperature around 37°C (98.6°F). To stay healthy, a human normally eats three balanced meals a day plus snacks.

Sharks in the main exhibit at SeaWorld Orlando are usually fed two days a week. The fish fed to the sharks at SeaWorld are filled with vitamin supplements to ensure a healthy and balanced diet. Because sharks are cold blooded, they may only eat 1% to 10% of their total body weight *per week*. In other words, a 2.75 m (9 ft.) sand tiger shark weighing 131 kg (289 lb.) may eat just 2 to 6 kg (4–13 lb.) a week. A dolphin that same size would eat that much or more every day. Sharks are often dubbed "eating machines." Yet when compared to endothermic or "warm blooded" animals, sharks seem to hardly eat at all. Sharks may go a month without eating at all, and there is speculation that basking sharks may go four or five months without food.

A shark's skeleton is made of cartilage, and its jaws don't hold its teeth in place like human jaws do. Some sharks have an incredible biting force, of up to 8,000 pounds per square inch (it takes only about 100 ppsi to break a human finger) so sharks naturally lose teeth when biting down on prey. Sharks replenish lost teeth throughout their lifetime. It is estimated that some sharks lose as many as 30,000 teeth in a lifetime.

Sharks have four or more rows of teeth. Back rows continuously move forward to replace lost ones and some species, like lemon sharks, can replace a lost tooth in eight days.

You might find discarded shark teeth washed up on a beach, although it would be rare to find a cookiecutter shark's teeth. Their teeth often end up in a cookiecutter's stomach. Scientists believe that cookiecutters lose an entire row of teeth at one time, and then they swallow and digest their own teeth. It is theorized that they do this because cookiecutters need high levels of calcium to survive, and digesting their teeth is a way to recycle this material.

The tooth of a great white.

Each shark species has a unique tooth pattern. Therefore, sharks can be identified and grouped by their teeth. Researchers can determine a shark's diet by examining its teeth. A great white shark, for example, has triangular teeth with serrated edges. The pointed tips of a great white indicate that it could consume marine creatures like fish.

A shark's jaws are loosely connected to the rest of the skull by cartilage and tendons at two points, allowing a shark to extend its jaws outward and forward. The teeth in the lower jaw of a sand tiger shark are like long, sharp forks. These teeth first impale and hold its prey. The upper jaw has knifelike teeth that then slice the flesh of the prey.

Port Jackson sharks hide at the bottom of coral reefs or tide pools. To take advantage of the wide variety of food in these areas, they have both sharp and flat teeth. Their sharp front teeth seize soft-bodied prey while their flat back teeth can crack open hard-shelled invertebrates. They probably grind food with their flat teeth, whereas most sharks swallow their food whole without chewing.

Port Jackson sharks have a combination of sharp and flat teeth. Their genus name, *Heterodontus*, means "different teeth."

41

Some sharks have highly specialized diets. The largest of all sharks, indeed the largest fish ever known, survives on the tiniest of foods.

The name "whale shark" may be confusing, but this massive fish has no connection to whales other than its great size. Although the whale shark has thousands of teeth in more than 300 rows, it no longer uses them. The mouth is terminal (in front of the body) whereas most sharks have mouths that are ventral (under the body behind the snout). Only the whale shark, megamouth, frilled sharks (*Chlamydoselachus* spp.) and some carpet sharks (family Parascylliidae) have terminal mouths.

The whale shark is a suction filter feeder, meaning it sucks in a huge volume of water rich with small sealife to eat. It can filter 1.5 million liters (400,000 gallons) of water an hour. The water is strained of tiny planktonic creatures through spongy tissues supported by cartilaginous rods between the whale shark's gill arches. Sometimes larger fishes, such as mackerels, anchovies, and tunas are sucked in as well.

Basking sharks, another large filter feeder, do not suck in water. They swim through it, with their huge mouths opened wide. Basking sharks have gill slits long enough to almost encircle their entire head, and with their mouths open they can filter 2,000 tons of water per hour while cruising at a steady speed of two knots (2.3 mph). Gill rakers, aligned along the inside of each of the five gill arches, are composed of thousands of tiny teeth that strain out planktonic animals. Mucus secreted in the pharynx supposedly coats the gill rakers to make them sticky. An entire ton of food has been found in one basking shark's stomach. Just as the teeth in basking sharks' mouths are constantly renewed, its gill rakers are shed and replaced as well. When the gill rakers are lost, some researchers believe basking sharks "hibernate" for months until the gill rakers grow back.

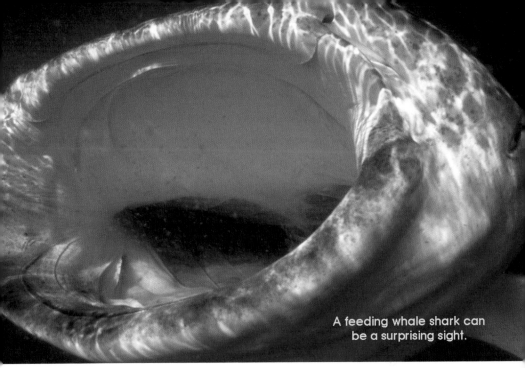

A feeding whale shark can be a surprising sight.

In 1976 a United States Navy research vessel was experimenting with a new type of sea anchor that had a pair of parachutes attached to it. When the anchor was lifted aboard, a mysterious creature was found wrapped around it. This newly discovered shark species was dubbed megamouth.

This 4.5-m (15-ft.) species is the third known filter feeding shark. Its open mouth exceeds 1 m (3.3 ft.) in width. The few that have been seen by humans were off Hawaii, Southern California, Australia, and Japan. Virtually nothing is known about the megamouth because only a few have been studied. Megamouths are known to follow shrimp species like *Thysanopoda pectinata*, however. In the daytime they seem to stay at depths below 1,000 m (3,300 ft.), but at night they rise to depths of around 150 m (490 ft.) in search of great groupings of shrimp. Their flabby bodies and relatively small gill slit openings suggest they are not as active as the other two filter feeding sharks. Megamouths have more than 100 rows of tiny teeth.

Sharks are extremely diverse animals, so it is no surprise that their behavior and diets also differ. The following pages offer a look at some of the sharks and their relatives found around the world.

Zebra or Australian Leopard Shark (*Stegostoma fasciatum*)
Distribution: Indo-Pacific areas such as Pakistan, Vietnam, the Philippines, China, Japan, and Australia.
Diet: Primarily molluscs and crustaceans but also some bony fishes.
Field Notes: Can probably reach a maximum size of 3.5 m (11.6 ft.) although its tail accounts for about half of the total body length.

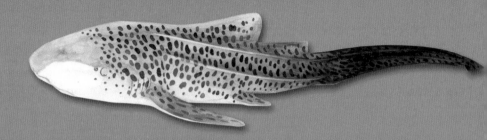

Blacktip Reef Shark (*Carcharhinus melanopterus*)
Distribution: Eastern Mediterranean Sea, Japan, China, and Australia.
Diet: Various bony fishes and invertebrates.
Field Notes: Along with whitetip and gray reef sharks, this active, powerful swimmer is one of the most common coral reef species.

Lemon Shark (*Negaprion brevirostris*)
Distribution: New Jersey to southern Brazil, the Bahamas, Gulf of Mexico, Senegal, southern Baja California to Ecuador.
Diet: Primarily fishes but also crustaceans and molluscs.
Field Notes: Lemon shark blood has a greater affinity for oxygen than most sharks, allowing them to live in oxygen-poor areas like mangroves. Their lemon yellow belly is more evident on younger specimens.

Scalloped Hammerhead (*Sphyrna lewini*)
Distribution: Coastal warm temperate and tropical seas around the world.
Diet: Various bony fishes, small sharks and rays, and invertebrates such as shrimp and crabs.
Field Notes: Although sometimes solitary, the scalloped hammerhead also can be found in large schools. Possibly the most numerous of all hammerhead species.

Brown or Sandbar Shark (*Carcharhinus plumbeus*)
Distribution: Southern Massachusetts to Florida, Gulf of Mexico, Brazil, Mediterranean and Red Seas, South Africa, Japan, Australia, and Madagascar.
Diet: Various bony fishes, small sharks and rays, and invertebrates such as octopuses and conch snails.
Field Notes: Called the "great migrator," sandbar sharks travel by the hundreds as they swim down the North Atlantic seaboard of the United States.

Sand tiger or Snaggletooth Shark (*Carcharias taurus*)
Distribution: Gulf of Maine to Florida, Gulf of Mexico, Red Sea, Indian Ocean, and Australia.
Diet: Various bony fishes, small sharks, squids, lobsters, and crabs.
Field Notes: Because sand tigers swim slowly through the water with multiple rows of sharp teeth exposed, they are often viewed as menacing. Unless provoked, however, this species is not considered a threat to humans.

Bonnethead (*Sphyrna tiburo*)
Distribution: Rhode Island to southern Brazil, Cuba, the Bahamas, Southern California to Ecuador.
Diet: Crustaceans including barnacles, octopuses, and small fishes.
Field Notes: A small member of the Sphyrnidae family with a maximum size up to 1.5 m (5 ft.). Seldom found alone, bonnethead sharks are usually found in small groups of 3 to 15 individuals.

Nurse Shark (*Ginglymostoma cirratum*)
Distribution: Rhode Island to Brazil, Gulf of Mexico, southern Baja California to Peru.
Diet: Bottom invertebrates such as shrimps, crabs and octopuses plus pufferfish, mullet, and stingrays.
Field Notes: Nurse sharks feed by sucking out the insides of hard-shelled creatures like conch snails. This feeding technique reminds some people of a baby mammal nursing from its mother.

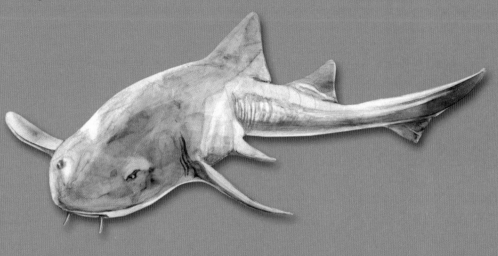

Horn Shark (*Heterodontus francisci*)
Distribution: Central California to Gulf of California, possibly Ecuador and Peru.
Diet: Sea urchins, crabs, and bony fishes.
Field Notes: In some parts of the world, people collect the dorsal spines of horn sharks and make them into jewelry.

Wobbegong *(Orectolobus japonicus)*
Distribution: Western South Pacific including Indonesia and Australia.
Diet: Bottom invertebrates and small fishes.
Field Notes: Wobbegongs are sluggish, bottom-dwelling sharks that rely on their exceptional camouflage to hide from enemies and gain food.

Leopard Shark *(Triakis semifasciata)*
Distribution: Oregon to Gulf of California and Mexico.
Diet: Fishes and their eggs, shrimps, crabs, and worms.
Field Notes: Known to form schools with brown smoothhound sharks (*Mustelus californicus*) and piked dogfish. Leopard sharks live 20 years or more in aquariums.

Blacktip Shark *(Carcharhinus limbatus)*
Distribution: Widespread in all tropical and subtropical waters.
Diet: Bony fishes, skates and rays, octopuses, and other sharks.
Field Notes: During feeding attacks, blacktip sharks have been known to dash upward through a school of fish and all the way out of the water.

48

Whitetip Reef Shark *(Triaenodon obesus)*
Distribution: Wide range in the Indo-Pacific including the Red Sea, South Africa, the Galápagos Islands, and Panama to Costa Rica.
Diet: Invertebrates and small fishes.
Field Notes: These sharks seem to be attracted to spearfishing and have been known to bite divers when fish blood is in the water. Otherwise, they are not considered dangerous.

Bull Shark *(Carcharhinus leucas)*
Distribution: Found along the continental coasts of all tropical and subtropical seas and some connected fresh water areas.
Diet: Broad spectrum of foods such as birds, bony fishes, skates and rays, sea turtles, crabs, and even other bull sharks.
Field Notes: This species belongs in the numerous and widespread Carcharhinidae family of sharks. Several Carcharhinidae members look similar to the bull shark, making it difficult to identify them in open water.

Smalltooth Sawfish *(Pristis pectinata)*
Distribution: Tropical Atlantic waters.
Diet: Bony fishes and invertebrates.
Field Notes: Sawfish are killed for their snouts which are sold as souvenirs. They are now protected by international law.

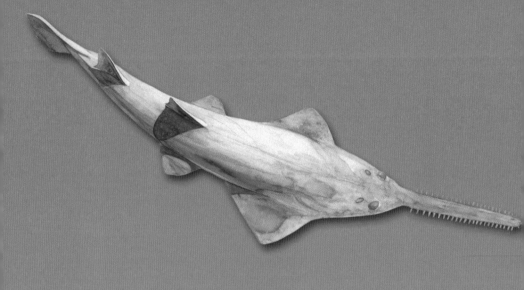

Blue-spotted Stingray *(Taeniura lymna)*
Distribution: Indo-Pacific tropics from southern Africa to the Solomon Islands.
Diet: Worms, shrimps, hermit crabs, and small fishes.
Field Notes: As opposed to most rays, this species has two venomous spines located near the end of its tail instead of at the tail base.

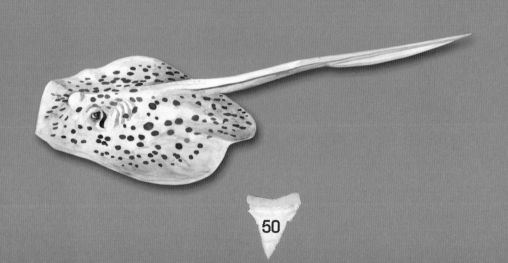

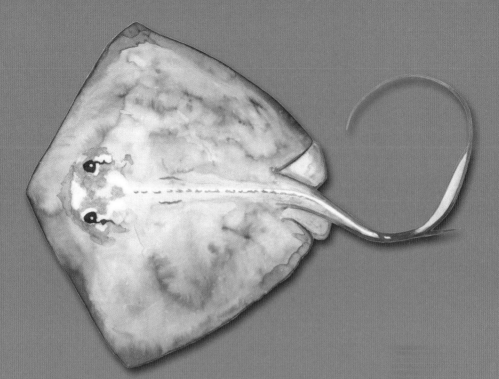

Southern Stingray *(Dasyatis americana)*
Distribution: Atlantic waters from New Jersey to Brazil.
Diet: Crabs, shrimps, worms, and bottom fishes.
Field Notes: SeaWorld has successfully bred southern stingrays. Southern stingray females have a gestation period from four to six months, depending upon the water temperature. Pups are about 20 cm (8 in.) wide at birth. As adults, some can reach a size up to 1.5 m (5 ft.) across.

Cownose Ray *(Rhinoptera bonasus)*
Distribution: Eastern United States to Brazil and the Gulf of Mexico.
Diet: Bottom invertebrates and small fishes.
Field Notes: These rays migrate huge distances in groups of as many as 6,000.

Saving Sharks & Rays

"If man doesn't learn to treat the oceans and the rain forest with respect, man will become extinct."

Peter Benchley, Author of "Jaws"

J ust how dangerous are sharks to people? As hard as it is to believe, more humans are killed every year by bees, elephants, dogs, or even pigs (i.e. wild pig attacks and farm accidents) than by sharks. In the United States, the animal that usually causes the most human deaths is deer! People get into an estimated 500,000 car accidents each year with deer, which result in approximately 100 human deaths. The percentage chance of a shark attack on a human is astronomically small. The chance of being struck by a lightning bolt is about 606,944 to one and about 100 to 200 people are killed in the United States every year by lightning. For the entire United States, there may be one or two reported shark related fatalities in an entire year.

Reported shark attacks are compiled and listed in the International Shark Attack File. According to the files, 62 unprovoked worldwide shark attacks occurred in 2006 (4 being fatal). In general, there are between 50 to 100 shark attacks and 5 to 10 fatalities reported per year. Without a doubt, humans are not part of a shark's normal diet. What's more, most people survive the attacks. This is even true with the notorious great white shark. California has the most great white attacks in the world, with 41 known attacks in 32 years, yet on the average there is only one fatality every eight years.

Left: Because they look fierce, sand tigers are feared and killed around the world. Like the nurse shark resting below it, a sand tiger shark is generally not dangerous to humans unless first provoked.
Above: Often, researchers must enter the domain of sharks to study them.

A shark fin jutting from the water often inspires fear, but is it justified?

There are many theories as to why sharks sometimes attack humans. An analysis of 1,000 worldwide attacks revealed that well over 50% of the attacks were not feeding related. Up to 60% of the injuries were slashes from the upper jaw teeth of various sharks. This behavior is typical of courtship advances by some male sharks. Also, a few sharks are believed to be territorial so a diver entering their space may be viewed as a threat.

Humans become prey by accident as well. Most shark attacks involve people handling hooked or snared sharks or spearfishermen handling wounded fish. Through sight and sound, a shark may confuse swimmers or divers for prey. A great white shark, for example, rushes toward its prey and attacks from beneath and behind. Swimmers, snorkelers, and surfers at the surface are more prone to attack than scuba divers beneath the water. At the surface, a human's silhouette may resemble that of a seal or sea lion; a favored prey of a great white.

Great white sharks are usually listed as the most dangerous shark for humans. But, 80% of reported shark attacks are in tropical waters where great whites are rare. The tropics are home to large, potentially dangerous species such as bull, tiger, lemon, and mako sharks. Given the extreme notoriety of great whites, it is possible that they are misidentified in many attacks.

An odd phenomenon occurs at False Bay, South Africa with great whites and boats. For some unknown reason, great whites attack more boats at False Bay than all other places in the world combined. A few of these boats were sunk and a great white actually leapt into a boat during one encounter.

Sometimes humans actually provoke or tease sharks to attack. Resting nurse sharks seem like a perfect photo opportunity to some divers, who may sit on these sharks for a picture. Although nurse sharks are generally sluggish, they may bite divers who harass or hurt them. Some human swimmers enter the water with open cuts or splash around the surface while playing. Like other top predators, sharks usually seek out weak or injured prey. Blood is a sign of injury, and so is the sound of thrashing. This is why many human activities in the water may attract and confuse sharks.

People are far more dangerous to sharks than sharks are to people. Sharks are killed and used for the most unusual things. The meat of the milk shark (*Rhizoprionodon acutus*) is believed by villagers to promote lactation in human females. Teeth of the Greenland shark are used by natives to cut hair and the shark skin is placed on the outside of their boats for added strength. Tiger shark vertebrae are crushed into the powder used by Japanese geisha girls. No part of a shark, however, is considered as economically valuable as its fins.

Shark skin can be abrasive, so it is used as a sandpaper (called shagreen) in some countries. If the denticles are removed, leather products of the finest quality can be manufactured.

Hawaiian villagers used shark teeth to create exotic tools ranging from cutting awls to weapons of war. These tiger shark teeth are still valued as jewelry, with the cost of a complete jaw averaging $200.

Shark fins can be worth up to $25 per pound, compared to shark meat which is valued at only $0.50 to $7 per pound. Finning operations drag sharks from the water, slice off their fins, and toss them back to die. Sharks are slaughtered by the millions just for their fins, which are used to make sharkfin soup. A delicacy in Asia, sharkfin soup can cost as much as $150 a bowl.

Medicinally, sharks are valuable to humans. Their liver oil is used for things ranging from vitamin supplements to hemorrhoid medication. Chondroiten, a substance found in shark cartilage, is a component of artificial skin used for treating burn patients and for acne medication. Anti-clotting compounds derived from sharks are more powerful than other commercial products, and shark corneas have been used as replacement corneas in people.

Sharks have an amazing immune system that can fight off many diseases. A substance called squalamine, found in the liver, stomach, and gall bladder of some dogfish, is believed to slow the growth of human brain tumors.

Recently, shark cartilage pills have been touted as a miracle cure for cancer. This claim is dubious to say the least. Studies done in 1998 showed that oral doses of shark cartilage had no effect on the growth of tumors in mice, and studies completed in 2005 on human cancer patients yielded similar results. It is the living cartilage of sharks that may affect a tumorous growth. In pill form, shark cartilage appears to be ineffective against cancer.

E very year, humans kill as many as 100 million sharks. This is especially alarming since sharks are apex ocean predators which mature and reproduce slowly. Female conger eels, which are low on the food chain, lay three to eight million eggs at one time. A Pacific sleeper shark was once found bearing 300 eggs, but only a few shark species may produce litters of more than 100 pups. The majority of species produce far fewer, leaving sharks vulnerable to the threat of overfishing.

Commercial fishing of sharks was sporadic in the United States until the 1970s. Then, the Federal government promoted sharks as an alternative to fishing for rapidly depleting stocks of bony fishes. By the late 1980s, a human "feeding frenzy" began on sharks. From 1986 to 1989, the commercial shark catch rose from 1,618 metric tons to 7,122 metric tons a year; a figure that did not include a huge increase in recreational shark fishing. Even worse, a study by the United Nations showed that for every shark that was taken on purpose, at least another was killed by accident.

Commercial catches had decreased 16% by 1990, indicating that sharks may have been removed far faster than they could reproduce. In 1993, the National Marine Fisheries Service (NMFS) established the Fishery Management Plan for Sharks of the Atlantic Ocean. The new law affected a 322 km (200 miles) area off the east coast of the United States, the Gulf of Mexico, and the Caribbean Sea. Permits were now required for commercial and charter boats that fished for sharks. Shark finning was banned and a yearly fishing quota of 2,450,000 kg (5.4 million lb.) was set for 22 large coastal species, seven small coastal species, and 10 pelagic species of sharks. The state of California also passed a law the same year, protecting the great white shark from harm.

According to the NMFS, those efforts were not enough. Many Atlantic shark populations plummeted perhaps 80% or more since the 1970s. In the spring of 1997, the NMFS cut the quota of large sharks to 1,285 metric tons; limited the catch of small coastal sharks; and banned the commercial harvest of whale, basking, great white, sand tiger, and bigeye sand tiger sharks (*Odontaspis noronhai*).

In the Pacific Ocean, shark finning actually increased in the 1990s. For example, between 1991 and 1998, the number of sharks caught by Hawaiian-based fisheries rose from 2,289 to 60,857 annually with upwards of 98% of these sharks being taken just for their fins. The United States finally extended its ban on shark finning to the Pacific with the Shark Finning Prohibition Act of 2000. This regulation makes it illegal for any federally regulated fishing vessel to take sharks without bringing back the entire carcass.

The international community has also seen the importance of protecting sharks. Through organizations such the United Nations, agreements like the International Plan of Action for Sharks and the Code of Conduct for Responsible Fishing promises to alleviate many of the problems facing sharks around the world.

Great white sharks are protected by law in several countries.

The piked dogfish may be the most numerous shark, since an estimated 27,000,000 were fished off the Massachusetts coast each year. Yet, many species such as the combtoothed lanternfish (*Etmopterus decacuspidatus*) are known only from a single specimen. The bizarre goblin shark (*Mitsukurina owstoni*), with its odd pointed snout, was not discovered until 1898. For many shark species, even basic information about them is rare.

Scientists would like to know more about sharks, especially their behaviors and learning capacities. In experiments, nurse and lemon sharks showed surprising abilities to learn, recognize, and remember different shapes and sound cues. Sharks are proving not to be the mindless creatures once depicted in the past.

Recent studies have also shed light on shark behavior. As the name would suggest, nervous sharks (*Carcharinus cautus*) are timid and skittish when approached by divers. Greenland sharks are so sluggish that they can actually be lifted out of the water without any resistance. But many other species readily investigate humans in the water as if out of curiosity.

An increasing area of study is in the development of shark repellents and protective dive gear. A chain mail suit made of 400,000 tiny, interlocking stainless steel rings (price tag: around $5,000) proved effective against the bites of smaller sharks. The opposite extreme of this is the *fundoshi,* a long, thin red cloth that female Japanese divers wear around their waists. The divers believe the fluttering tail may scare some sharks away or divert the shark into biting the cloth. One especially promising device is called the Shark Screen. The Shark Screen is like a plastic sleeping bag that floats in the water. Most shark attacks on humans occur on easier targets like arms and legs. A person inside the Shark Screen has the advantage of appearing as one large mass to a shark, with no easy targets to bite. Also, body chemicals and blood cannot escape into the water to attract sharks.

The SeaWorld Adventure Parks and the Hubbs/SeaWorld Research Institute study sharks and educates the public on their vital role in the ocean environment.

Researchers at SeaWorld study growth rates, blood chemistry, and reproduction in sharks. A milestone for shark breeding occurred at SeaWorld Orlando in 1995 when brown shark pups were conceived and born in the main aquarium. This was the first time that such an event happened in the United States. SeaWorld San Diego was the first aquarium to successfully breed Pacific blacktip sharks. SeaWorld recently assisted the NMFS and Albion College with the most extensive study of the reproduction of collected nurse sharks ever undertaken. Ultrasound and intrauterine endoscopy were used to document the pregnancies of two nurse sharks that were brought to SeaWorld Orlando. When the tests were completed, both the females and their offspring were tagged and released back to the wild where their mating activities were originally witnessed and filmed.

The education team at SeaWorld conducts dozens of classes, tours, camps, and hands-on encounters that show guests the importance of sharks. Shamu TV,® a free satellite and distance learning program, provides classrooms and homes around the world an up-close look into the world of sharks and other animals.

The SeaWorld & Busch Gardens Conservation Fund (SWBGCF) supports projects to protect sharks around the world. Little information exists, for example, on the Puget Sound's sixgill shark population. The SWBGCF has funded studies on the migration patterns, population status, sizes, and age/genders of these mysterious sharks.

In China and Central and South America, the SWBGCF and WildAid's Shark Conservation Program teamed up to elevate the importance of conserving shark populations from finning practices. Numerous laws have been strengthened to protect sharks, and there has been a decrease in the amount of shark consumption in key Asian countries thanks to this effort.

SeaWorld and the Hubbs/SeaWorld Research Institute tagged whale sharks in Baja California and monitored their migration patterns to learn more about them.

In Belize, the Meso-American Reef area is being threatened by unregulated tourism, over-fishing, and agricultural runoff. A grant by the SWBGCF is helping to bring neighboring countries together to discuss ways to conserve this vital area. Such funding helps to protect shark species, such as the whale shark, as well as all of the other marine life found in this the second largest barrier reef system in the world.

Sharks have a value far beyond human economics. Perhaps the greatest challenge with shark conservation is convincing people of the need to protect them.

Often sharks eat sick and weak prey. This actually improves the gene pool for the stronger, healthier individuals that go on to reproduce. Shark overfishing removes this vital link in the delicate balance of the ocean ecosystem. When sharks were overfished around Australia, the octopus population increased dramatically. The octopus then preyed heavily on spiny lobsters and decreased that population, causing hardship to local lobster fishermen. By destroying sharks, humans may unwittingly remove a key predator that keeps the populations of other creatures healthy.

Sharks in the *Somniosus* genus stay in the chilly Arctic waters all year round. The bigeye houndshark (*Lago omanensis*) has been found at the bottom of the Red Sea, some 2,195 m (7,200 ft.) deep. Blue sharks have one of the largest ranges of all marine vertebrates. They can be found throughout the world in temperate and tropical oceans and blue sharks migrate huge distances. Tagging studies have shown that one blue shark swam 4,344 km (2,700 miles) in four months. From shallow tide pool waters to depths thousands of meters below the ocean's continental slopes, sharks have a nearly cosmopolitan distribution.

A new trend for thrill-seeking divers is to swim with sharks. Shark dive programs are growing in popularity off places like the Hawaiian and Caribbean islands. To attract sharks to a dive site, some tour operators heavily chum the area with dead fish. Scientists and legislators are debating whether such practices are wise; chumming the water may make sharks dependent on humans for food and increase the likelihood of attacks.

Another way to see sharks is to visit marine life parks. At shark displays, millions of people each year gain a rare opportunity to see sharks up-close. Learning about these amazing animals may be the best hope to educate people on the value sharks have to us all.

Left and right: Educational programs at SeaWorld allow guests to get up-close with sharks in safe and exciting ways.

65

Classification

Superorder Selachii

Order Hexanchiformes
  Family Hexanchidae (cowsharks, six-gill and seven-gill sharks)
  Family Chlamydoselachidae (frilled sharks)

Order Squaliformes
  Family Squalidae (dogfishes)
  Family Echinorhinidae (bramble sharks)
  Family Oxynotidae (rough sharks)

Order Pristiophoriformes
  Family Pristiophoridae (sawsharks)

Order Squatiniformes
  Family Squatinidae (angelsharks)

Order Heterodontiformes
  Family Heterodontidae (horn sharks)

Order Orectolobiformes
  Family Orectolobidae (wobbegong sharks)
  Family Ginglymostomatidae (nurse sharks)
  Family Rhincodontidae (whale sharks)*
  Family Parascylliidae (collared carpet sharks)
  Family Brachaeluridae (blind sharks)
  Family Hemiscylliidae (bamboo sharks)
  Family Stegostomatidae (zebra sharks)

Order Lamniformes
  Family Odontaspididae (sand tiger sharks)
  Family Mitsukurinidae (goblin shark)
  Family Lamnidae (mackerel sharks)
  Family Cetorhinidae (basking sharks)
  Family Alopiidae (thresher sharks)
  Family Pseudocarchariidae (crocodile sharks)
  Family Megachasmidae (megamouth shark)

Order Carcharhiniformes
  Family Scyliorhinidae (catsharks)
  Family Proscylliidae (ribbontail catsharks)
  Family Pseudotriakidae (false catsharks)
  Family Leptochariidae (barbeled houndsharks)
  Family Triakidae (smoothhound sharks)
  Family Hemigaleidae (weasel sharks)
  Family Carcharhinidae (requiem sharks)
  Family Sphyrnidae (hammerhead sharks)

Superorder Batoidea

Order Rajiformes
  Family Rajidae (skates)
  Family Rhinobatidae (guitarfish)

Order Torpediniformes
  Family Torpedinidae (electric rays)

Order Pristidae
  Family Pristidae (sawfish)

Order Myliobatiformes
  Family Dasyatidae (stingrays)
  Family Myliobatidae (eagle rays)
  Family Mobulidae (devil rays)
  Family Rhinopteridae (cownosed rays)
  Family Urolophidae (round stingrays)
  Family Gymnuridae (butterfly rays)
  Family Potamotrygonidae (river rays)

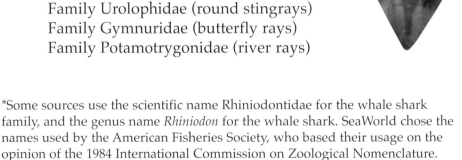

*Some sources use the scientific name Rhiniodontidae for the whale shark family, and the genus name *Rhiniodon* for the whale shark. SeaWorld chose the names used by the American Fisheries Society, who based their usage on the opinion of the 1984 International Commission on Zoological Nomenclature.

Bibliography

Cafiero, Gaetano and Maddalena Jahoda. *Shark Myth and Reality*. Charlotteville: Thomasson-Grant, Inc., 1994.

Compagno, Leonard J. V. *FAO Species Catalogue, Vol. 4, An Annotated and Illustrated Catalogue of Sharks Species Known to Date*. Rome: United Nations Press, 1984.

Compagno, Leonard J. V., Kim Holland, John E. McCoster, and Colin Simpfendorfer. *Reader's Digest Explores Sharks*. New York: Reader's Digest Association, Inc., 1998.

Coulombe, Deborah A. *The Seaside Naturalist*. New York: Prentice Hall Press, 1987.

Dixon, Douglas, Barry Cox and R.J.G. Savage. *The Macmillan Illustrated Encyclopedia of Dinosaurs and Prehistoric Animals*. London: Marshalls Edition Limited, 1988.

Ellis, Richard and John E. McCosker. *Great White Shark*. Stanford: HarperCollins Publishers, 1991.

Johnson, R. H. *Sharks of Tropical and Temperate Seas*. Singapore: Les Editions du Pacifique, 1990.

Klimley, A. Peter and David G. Ainley. *Great White Sharks*. San Diego: Academic Press, 1996.

Last, P. R. and J. D. Stevens. *Sharks and Rays of Australia*. Australia: Csiro, 1994.

Lemonick, Michael D. "Under Attack." *Time* 150 (6), August 11, 1997, pp. 59–64.

Michael, Scott W. Reef *Sharks & Rays of the World*. Monterey: Sea Challengers, 1993.

Springer, Victor G. and Joy P. Gold. *Sharks in Question. The Smithsonian Answer Book*. Washington D.C.: Smithsonian Institute Press, 1989.

Taylor, Geoff. *Whale Sharks: The Giants of Ningaloo Reef*. Sydney: HarperCollins Publishers, Inc., 1994.

Taylor, Leighton. *Sharks and Rays*. China: Leefung-Asco Printers, 1997.

Books for Young Readers

Arnold, Caroline. *Watch Out For Sharks!* New York: Clarion Books, 1991.

Bannister, Keith. *A Look Inside Sharks and Rays.* New York: Reader's Digest Association, Inc., 1995.

Cerullo, Mary M. *Sharks. Challengers of the Deep.* New York: Cobblehill, 1993.

Chinery, Michael. *Life Story. Shark.* Mahwah, New Jersey: Troll Associates, 1991.

Gibbons, Gail. *Sharks.* New York: Holiday House, 1992.

le Bloas, Renee and Jerome Julienne. *The Shark. Silent Hunter.* Watertown, Massachusetts: Charlesbridge Publishing, 1998.

Maestro, Betsy. *A Sea Full of Sharks.* New York: Scholastic, Inc. 1990.

Markle, Sandra. *Outside and Inside Sharks.* New York: Atheneum, 1996.

Maynard, Christopher. *Infomania Sharks.* Cambridge, Massachusetts, 1997.

McGovern, Ann. *Questions and Answers About Sharks.* New York: Scholastic Inc., 1995.

Pope, Joyce. *Pockets. Sharks.* New York: DK Publishing, Inc., 1997.

Web Sites

Animal information from SeaWorld and Busch Gardens
SeaWorld.org
BuschGardens.org

American Zoo and Aquarium Association
aza.org

International Shark Attack Files
www.flmnh.ufl.edu/fish/Sharks/ISAF/ISAF.htm

FishBase: A Global Information System on Fishes
fishbase.org

SeaWorld & Busch Gardens Conservation Fund
SWBGConservationFund.org

Glossary

anal fin — the median fin located on the underside of a fish, between the anus and the caudal fin. (Not all fishes have an anal fin.)

bony fish — any fish of the class Osteichthyes, characterized by a skeleton of bone.

bycatch — nontarget animals caught during a fishing operation.

cartilage — a type of tough, flexible connective tissue. Cartilage composes the skeleton of sharks and all very young vertebrates.

caudal fin — the tail fin.

Chondrichthyes (kon-DRIK-theez) — a scientific class of fishes that have jaws, paired fins, paired nostrils, and a skeleton composed of cartilage.

dermal denticle — a toothlike scale consisting of an outer layer of enamel, dentine, and a pulp cavity.

dorsal fin — a fin on the back of a whale or fish.

finning — the practice of removing only a shark's fins, which are used in sharkfin soup.

gill slits — slitlike openings through which water leaves a shark's gills

oviparous — a mode of reproduction by producing eggs that hatch outside the mother's body. (In sharks, eggs are fertilized internally.)

ovoviviparous — a mode of reproduction by producing eggs that are fertilized internally and retained within the body until they are developed. Embryos are nourished by a yolk sac formed prior to fertilization.

pectoral fins — the paired fins towards the front of a fish's body.

pelvic fins — the paired fins on the underside of a fish's body, behind the pectoral fins.

viviparous — a mode of reproduction by producing eggs that are fertilized internally and retained within the body until they are developed. Embryos are nourished by a direct connection with tissues of the mother.

Goals of the SeaWorld & Busch Gardens Education Department

Based on a long-term commitment to education, SeaWorld and Busch Gardens strive to provide an enthusiastic, imaginative, and intellectually stimulating atmosphere to help students and guests develop a lifelong appreciation, understanding, and stewardship for our environment. Specifically, the goals are...

- To instill in students and guests of all ages an appreciation for science and a respect for all living creatures and habitats.
- To conserve our valuable natural resources by increasing awareness of the interrelationships of humans and the environment.
- To increase students' and guests' basic competencies in science, math, and other disciplines.
- To be an educational resource to the world.

"For in the end we will conserve only what we love. We will love only what we understand. We will understand only what we are taught." — B. Dioum

Want more information?

SeaWorld and Busch Gardens has books, teacher guides, posters, and videos available on a variety of animals and topics. For more information, visit the SeaWorld/Busch Gardens Animal Information Database at
www.seaworld.org
or *www.buschgardens.org*

Anheuser-Busch Adventure Parks

SeaWorld Orlando
(800) 406–2244
7007 SeaWorld Dr.
Orlando, FL 32821

SeaWorld San Antonio
(210) 523–3606
10500 SeaWorld Dr.
San Antonio, TX 78251

SeaWorld San Diego
(800) 380–3202
500 SeaWorld Dr.
San Diego, CA 92109

Discovery Cove
(877) 4–DISCOVERY
6000 Discovery Cove Way
Orlando, FL 32821

Busch Gardens Tampa Bay
(813) 987–5555
P.O. Box 9158
Tampa, FL 33674-9158

Busch Gardens Williamsburg
(757) 253–3000
One Busch Gardens Boulevard
Williamsburg, VA 23187-8785